To

From

Date

REBUILDING YOUR LIFE

Lessons From The Life And Mission of Nehemiah

REFLECTION WORKBOOK

THE CORNERSTONE PUBLISHING

JOSEPH OLOWE

REBUILDING YOUR LIFE - REFLECTION WORKBOOK

Paperback ISBN: 978-1-944652-72-2

Published By:
Cornerstone Publishing
A division of Cornerstone Creativity Group LLC
Info@thecornerstonepublishers.com
www.thecornerstonepublishers.com

For booking to speak at your next event or to order bulk copies of this book please use information below:

P. O Box 10499
El Paso, TX 79995
1-800-561-9170 or +1 915-478-8807
www.drjosepholowe.com | info@drjosepholowe.com

DEDICATION

This book is dedicated to my prophet, father and revered mentor in the Lord **Bishop David Oyedepo**, whom I have never met personally but has impacted my life in many ways beyond words. I will forever be grateful for your leadership in the body of Christ and for being a perfect example for us to emulate.

ACKNOWLEDGMENTS

I will like to appreciate my savior Jesus Christ from whom all blessings flow. My sincere gratitude to my wife and partner in ministry, Omolade for her relentless pursuit of excellence for our family first and ministry.

To my children Olamide, Simi and Dare who have given me an opportunity to practice what I am preaching.

To my ministry team, first to my able editor who I consider as a gift from heaven to me, Pastor Joseph Ola and to Daniel Emonido who I refer to as mighty Danny, for all the divine graphics; many thanks.

To Pastor Gbenga Showunmi and his professional team at Cornerstone Publishing, thank you for making this dream come true.

To a good friend of mine, Pastor David Olayemi — the first man apart from my family, who sincerely believed in my writing gift and encouraged me to pursue my dream — may the God of heaven never forget your labor of love

CONTENTS

Dedication.....5

Acknowledgments.....7

Introduction.....13

Day 1: The Month of Chisleu.....15

Day 2: I Am Nehemiah.....18

Day 3: Prayer of Nehemiah.....23

Day 4: Planning For Rebuilding.....26

Day 5: A Thorough Assessment.....29

Day 6: First Thing First.....32

Day 7: Condition of The Heart.....35

Day 8: Common Areas of Rebuilding In Life.....38

Day 9: Seeking God First.....41

Day 10: Favor Factor.....44

Day 11: Power of Diligence....47

Day 12: Power of Perseverance....50

Day 13: Power of Prayer....53

Day 14: Building or Rebuilding A Relationship....56

Day 15: Wisdom....58

Day 16: Power of Love....61

Day 17: The Power of Forgiveness....64

Day 18: United Prayer....67

Day 19: Power of Fasting....70

Day 20: Building or Rebuilding A Family....73

Day 21: Stable Homes....75

Day 22: Building Godly Character....79

Day 23: Godly Training....82

Day 24: Godly Discipline....84

Day 25: Prayer As The Master Key....87

Day 26: Building or Rebuilding A Business....90

Day 27: Building Integrity....92

Day 28: Developing Knowledge of Witty Inventions And Wise Planning....95

Day 29: Treating People Right....98

Day 30: Faithfulness In Financial Matters With God............101

Day 31: The Power of Continuous Training And Improvement..........104

Day 32: The Bondage Breaker..........107

Day 33: The Effect of Socialization..........109

Day 34: The Problem With Bad Company..........112

Day 35: Time to Every Purpose..........114

Day 36: Being Accountable..........117

Day 37: Neglecting Evil Behavior..........120

Day 38: Health Matters..........123

Day 39: Enemies of Progress..........126

Day 40: Who Was Tobiah?..........128

Day 41: Who Was Geshem?..........130

Day 42: The Plains of Ono..........132

Day 43: Tactic #1: Mockery..........134

Day 44: Tactic #2: Anger And Conspiracy..........136

Day 45: Tactic #3: Tiredness And Loss of Vigor..........138

Day 46: Tactic #4: Fear of The Adversary..........141

Day 47: Tactic #5: Propaganda As A Tool of Manipulation..........144

Day 48: Tactic #6: False Prophecy And Distraction..............146

Day 49: Under A Better Covenant...149

Day 50: Kingdom Stewardship...152

Day 51: Praise And Worship As A Weapon.............................155

Day 52: The Month of Elul...157

INTRODUCTION

The most common thing in life is CHANGE. The weather changes. Leadership changes. Policies change. And we — yes — we also change! Our lives do change as a result of decisions and indecisions. Some changes are trivial; others are drastic.

To cause a life-changing transformation in a child, spouse, family, job situation or even a nation involves a drastic but God-focused intervention. This was what Nehemiah did to restore the glory of God back to Jerusalem, and anyone looking for such a change can engage like Nehemiah did. Therefore, this devotional is about raising a generation of restorers like Nehemiah.

As you sincerely and holistically look at your life, community or church, you are likely to find areas that bear a close resemblance to the broken walls of Jerusalem – areas that are either not fully reflecting the promises and expectations of God for His children, or that have become outright sources of concern and reproach because they are completely broken down or in total disarray. This is why the Holy Spirit has caused this book to be written at this moment.

Like the wall of Jerusalem, your life is very important to God. And it doesn't matter how much damage that has been done to it or how long the damage has taken, it can be rebuilt and made even more glorious. All that is needed is a firm belief in the expertise of God, the Master-builder, the willingness to cooperate with Him and the commitment to the process of rebuilding, which is the central focus of this book.

More cheeringly, as you will find in the practical application of the exploit of Nehemiah contained in this book, there is no aspect of your life that cannot be built or rebuilt with the wisdom, power and guidance of the Holy Spirit. In other words, no area of your life should be in doldrums. Every part of it matters to God and He wants you to prosper, flourish and excel in each of the components (3 John 2). So, whether it is your spiritual, physical, financial, marital, emotional or professional life that you want to build or rebuild, God is reaching out to you through this book with a message of hope and that it will receive and respond to His quickening intervention. He has done it before (recall the story of the dry bones in Ezekiel 37) and He's willing and able to do it again – as long as you can cooperate with Him by following the principles outlined in this volume.

HOW TO USE THIS BOOK

This book has been prepared to be read on a day-to-day basis, over a period of 52 days. Prayerfully read through the message and Bible references for each day and meditate on them. Welcome to the journey of rebuilding your life!

Happy rebuilding!

Day 1

THE MONTH OF CHISLEU

"The words of Nehemiah the son of Hachaliah. And it came to pass in the month Chisleu, in the twentieth year, as I was in Shushan the palace." (Nehemiah 1:1)

Nehemiah had been in exile for a number of years before he embarked on the historic process of rebuilding the wall of Jerusalem. Remarkably, the quest began with certain questions he asked about the city of Jerusalem and its inhabitants. Moreover, despite the dismal and heartbreaking report that he got, he did not just begin to rebuild, he chose to be strategic by taking certain important steps and waiting for the most favorable time.

This is your own month of Chisleu. So, get into the rebuilding mode with the following exercises:

1. How many years had Nehemiah been in exile before starting to rebuild the wall of Jerusalem and what does this mean for you personally?

2. That Nehemiah began his quest in the month of Chisleu was no coincidence. What month is Chisleu in the Jewish calendar and of what significance is it?

3. Worthy of note is that Nehemiah's noble achievement began with some crucial questions he asked Hanani concerning the Jews that had escaped, which were left of the captivity, and concerning Jerusalem. Take a cue from this and do a complete inventory of your life to identify areas of lifelessness, crisis, failure, reproach, breakdown, or lack of progress. Write them out in sincerity:

a.

b.

c.

d.

e.

4. What specific turnaround do you wish to experience in each of the areas outlined above?

a.

b.

c.

d.

5. Make a deal with God in prayer (possibly, with fasting), showing your readiness for life-transforming changes in the identified areas of lifelessness and asking Him to guide you through.

Day 2

I AM NEHEMIAH

"And it came to pass, when I heard these words, that I sat down and wept, and mourned certain days, and fasted, and prayed before the God of heaven." (Nehemiah 1:4)

Let's face it – rebuilding is never an easy task. In fact, it is a well-known saying that it is much easier to pull down than to build up, to fall than to climb. Nehemiah knew about this, but it's not just about knowing – his peculiar circumstance and the situation around him all pointed to the impossibility or, at least, extreme difficulty of what he was embarking upon. Everything surrounding the rebuilding assignment he was to begin - the task, the target, the tools and timing – threatened to be a major challenge for him. Yet, Nehemiah considered the ultimate benefits of the assignment above the expected challenges – a major trait of all winners and champions in life.

Note also that Nehemiah was not the only privileged Jew in captivity; nor was he in any way more disadvantaged by the state of things in Jerusalem than any other person. He could have simply looked away from the situation; but he, like many other heroes and heroines of faith, chose to be God's instrument of change in his generation. God is a Spirit and for Him to fulfill His purposes in the physical realm always seeks a human that will make himself or herself available for His use. Look within and around you – there's so much to be built or rebuilt in your life, family, church, community and nation. So many broken walls and damaged lives to be made whole again. Who else will God use to repair the breach when you can make yourself available? Who else can initiate the process for the new beginning?

Are you a Nehemiah? The following exercises will guide you:

1. What does the name, "Nehemiah" mean?

2. How did Nehemiah justify the meaning of his name?

3. God is seeking Nehemiahs in this generation. In what ways can you choose to be a Nehemiah today in your life, family, church, community or nation? Write them down below:

I will be a Nehemiah in my own life by________________________

____

I will be a Nehemiah in my home by__________________________

I will be a Nehemiah in my church by____________________

I will be a Nehemiah in my community/nation by___________

4. To build or rebuild requires counting the cost, as well as anticipating challenges – just as Nehemiah did. This will help you to be better prepared and not get discouraged when the challenges come. So, look again at exercise 3 above and identify the following in the areas you have chosen to build or rebuild:

What is the task? (What exactly do you want to build or rebuild?)

In your life____

____

In your home______________________________________

____

In your church_____________________________________

In your community/nation___________________________

____

5. Who are your targets? (Who are the people that may be affected by or instrumental to the task you want to carry out?)

In your life____

____

In your home_______________________________________

____

In your church______________________________________

In your community/nation____________________________

____

6. What tools or resources will you need to accomplish your task and how do you plan to get them? (Remembering that you have an all-sufficient God).

In your life____

____

In your home_______________________________________

____

In your church______________________________________

In your community/nation____________________________

____

7. How much time would you need to accomplish your task? (Set a practical deadline for yourself!)

In your life____

____

In your home____

____

In your church_______________________________________

In your community/nation____________________________

____

8. Knowing beforehand that every building, rebuilding or recovery process must come with certain challenges or prices to pay, it is wisdom to anticipate possible challenges and map out strategies to combat them. Sincerely outline some challenges that may come with your decision and the steps you will take to tackle them.

Possible Challenge	**Personal Resolve**
1.	
2.	
3.	
4.	
5.	

Day 3

PRAYER OF NEHEMIAH

"And said, I beseech thee, O Lord God of heaven, the great and terrible God, that keepeth covenant and mercy for them that love him and observe his commandments:" (Nehemiah 1:5)

As all who have succeeded in the battles of life and destiny can testify, no one who wants to accomplish anything meaningful or lasting can do without prayer. This is not just because there are situations and needs that are beyond human ability but also because there are forces that are bent on making every potential achiever to become a failure in their life and in their God-given assignments. Nehemiah, just like Jesus Christ, Paul the apostle, John Knox and many others who have changed the course of history, knew this truth; hence he did not embark on his mission of rebuilding without first seeking the face and favor of God. And, in his prayer points, we find vital secrets of an effective prayer which anyone who wants to build or rebuild anything significant can emulate. You too can pray like Nehemiah. Attempt the following:

1. Identify, at least, five essential lessons that you can derive from Nehemiah's prayer points.

a.

b.

c.

d.

e.

2. Nehemiah, in his prayer, reminded God of His words. Can you identify, at least, five promises of God pertaining to your situation that you can remind Him of in prayer?

a.

b.

c.

d.

e.

3. Being specific about his requests was one major reason that Nehemiah's prayer got results. You too can do same. Write out five specific things you want God to do for you – three, within this month; and two before the end of the year.

MY PRAYER REQUESTS

This month

a.

b.

c.

Before end of year

d.

e.

Day 4

PLANNING FOR REBUILDING

"And it came to pass in the month Nisan, in the twentieth year of Artaxerxes the king, that wine was before him: and I took up the wine, and gave it unto the king. Now I had not been beforetime sad in his presence." (Nehemiah 2:1)

Nehemiah was a good planner and strategist. We have noted how he did not just rush to commence the rebuilding process – he waited for the opportune time: the month of Nisan, which, like Chisleu, is a significant month in the Jewish calendar. And while he waited, he kept himself busy by planning and fashioning out the strategies that would ensure the success of his assignment. His planning involved a number of stages, which you can learn from in your rebuilding efforts. His methodical approach also reflected the seriousness with which he considered the task ahead of him. This is important for you to succeed in the rebuilding and recovery process.

Follow the example of Nehemiah with these exercises:

1. What month is the month of Nisan in the Jewish calendar and what is its significance?

2. The first stage of Nehemiah's plans involves a number of instructive steps or considerations. Can you identify these?

3. Considering his important position as the butler of King Artaxerxes, Nehemiah could have delegated the responsibility of rebuilding the wall to Hanani who had given him the report that propelled him to action, but he chose not to. Why do you think he made this decision, and what does it tell you about the process of rebuilding your life?

4. Using the example of Nehemiah, what do you think is the place of each of the following factors to your rebuilding process:

Communication

Authority

Budgeting

Security

In what practical ways will you apply the listed factors and make them work for you as you rebuild?

Day 5

A THOROUGH ASSESSMENT

"When Sanballat the Horonite, and Tobiah the servant, the Ammonite, heard of it, it grieved them exceedingly that there was come a man to seek the welfare of the children of Israel." (Nehemiah 2:10)

The next stage of Nehemiah's preparation consisted of a number of steps or factors that bordered on assessment of his level of preparedness. These steps included identification of his adversaries, getting himself involved in the situation on ground in Jerusalem, watching his tongue, taking a more critical look at the task before him, constituting a team of helpers, and setting his expectations at the beginning. All these were to help furnish and fortify himself with all that would keep him focused on the task ahead until it was accomplished. This pattern of assessment is exactly what you too must engage in, so that you will have a truly productive rebuilding quest.

These exercises will guide your assessment efforts:

1. It is important to know your adversaries, so you can know how best to handle them. What are those personal weaknesses that tend to weaken or frustrate your plan for progress in your spiritual, marital, academic or professional life? List them here.

Spiritual life

Marital life

Academic pursuit

Professional life

2. What decisive decisions are you making to stop these personal weaknesses from stopping you this time around?

3. The enemies that Nehemiah identified were physical, human enemies. You could also be in a similar situation. Are there individuals who usually constitute a clog in your wheel of progress, or who are likely to be so as you begin to rebuild your life? (Note that these include both those who are likely to oppose your moves or who are going to ridicule you or try to discourage you).

a.

b.

c.

d.

e.

4. Nehemiah personally got involved in the rebuilding process. He, in fact, took the lead by going to Jerusalem himself to spend some days, in order to get fully acquainted with his mission. Bearing in mind that you are the Nehemiah in your life, family, church and community, make a pledge to do all within your capability and God-given grace to effect the desired change, regardless of what others may be doing.

I____________(insert your name) pledge to make the rebuilding of__________(insert the area of life you want to build/ rebuild) my personal responsibility. I will do all I can within my personal capability and the grace of God bestowed on me to make it a success. So help me God.

5. While making the rebuilding a principally personal responsibility, you still need the support of a few other like-minds, just like Nehemiah did. List names of individuals you will need to guide and support you in your task.

a.

b.

c.

d.

e.

Day 6

FIRST THING FIRST

"Then said I unto them, Ye see the distress that we are in, how Jerusalem lieth waste, and the gates thereof are burned with fire: come, and let us build up the wall of Jerusalem, that we be no more a reproach." (Nehemiah 2:17)

While Nehemiah made plans to commence the rebuilding of the wall of Jerusalem, he had one fundamental motive – to remove the reproach on God's people. It was not to seek personal interest or gain. This noble objective of seeking to glorify God by alleviating the burdens of His people formed a solid foundation for Nehemiah's exploits. It significantly affected his approach and attitude to the task of rebuilding. You also need a sure foundation on which to rebuild your life. That Foundation is Jesus. A life without Christ will always be a life of reproach and crisis. Jesus made it clear to Nicodemus that except any man is born again, he cannot see the kingdom of God, which also means that he cannot have his life rebuilt.

The following exercises will guide you to do the first thing first, like Nehemiah:

1. Have you been born again? YES/NO

2. If your answer is YES to the above, state when it happened. If you answered NO, go to exercise four.____________________

____

3. Briefly describe your salvation (born again) experience below.

HOW I BECAME BORN AGAIN

4. If you answered NO to exercise one, you can become a child of God today through Jesus. Or perhaps, you had made Christ your Savior before but currently uncertain of your right standing with God. Understand that He is a God of another chance. Let's do it right now. You can say these words:

> Lord Jesus, come in to my life today. I confess You before men that You become my Lord and Savior; I choose to follow You from now on. I give my life to You. Thank You for Your love for me. Amen

5. Beginning a relationship with Christ is certainly a great experience, but it's one you have to nurture so it will continue to grow. These three resources have been known to be of immense help to those seeking to maintain and enrich their relationship with

Christ – prayer, the Holy Bible, fellowship with fellow believers. Write what you'll do with each in the spaces below:

Prayer____

The Holy Bible____

Fellowship with fellow believers___________________________

Day 7

CONDITION OF THE HEART

"And they said unto me, The remnant that are left of the captivity there in the province are in great affliction and reproach: the wall of Jerusalem also is broken down, and the gates thereof are burned with fire. And it came to pass, when I heard these words, that I sat down and wept, and mourned certain days, and fasted, and prayed before the God of heaven." (Nehemiah 1:3-4)

We have identified that Nehemiah's motive for rebuilding was to bring glory to God by tackling the reproachful situation that Jerusalem and its inhabitants were in. He was not driven by desire for self-recognition or vainglory. So, the condition of his heart was fully attuned to doing the will of God. No wonder, he got sufficient divine backing. When we compare the success he recorded with the failure recorded by the builders of the Tower of Babel, as well as King Amaziah, we realize one truth that is crucial to the success of our rebuilding efforts: The condition of our heart is very important to God, especially when we are soliciting His help to overcome our challenges and limitations.

Try the following exercises to position your heart to attract divine visitation and support upon you as you rebuild:

1. What is your primary purpose in embarking on the rebuilding quest?

2. In what ways will the name of the Lord be glorified in this assignment? Highlight them below:

3. Identify at least two individuals or groups of individuals in the Scripture whose exploits ended in failure and the lessons you can learn from them.

Name of Individual(s)	**Lesson from Their Failure**

4. Aside from Nehemiah, identify any three other personalities in the Scripture who did exploits for the glory of God and received commendation.

a.

b.

c.

What lessons can you learn from these people as you rebuild?

Day 8

COMMON AREAS OF REBUILDING IN LIFE

"Then I told them of the hand of my God which was good upon me; as also the king's words that he had spoken unto me. And they said, Let us rise up and build. So they strengthened their hands for this good work." (Nehemiah 2:18)

One of the essential lessons we learn from the accomplishment of Nehemiah is that every area of our lives can be built or rebuilt, with a combination of personal commitment and divine support. One common area that every one of us must build or rebuild at one time or the other in the course of our life is our career. And the dominant message from the experience of Nehemiah is that regardless of all that may have happened in the past – failure, frustration, disappointment, victimization, bankruptcy, ridicule – you can still fulfill God's purpose for your life by dreaming again.

Prep up your career prospects with the following exercises:

1. What was that KEY element that enabled Nehemiah to rebuild the wall of Jerusalem, which you must have to successfully build or rebuild a career?

2. Why do you need the Holy Spirit's help in building or rebuilding your career?

3. Cite, at least, two Scripture references that state how the Holy Spirit can be of help to your career success.

a.

b.

4. Nehemiah clearly had a vision of what he wanted to achieve before embarking on the quest of rebuilding the wall. Can you recall two more persons in the Scripture who had a dream of where they were going in life before getting there?

a.

b.

5. Identify five lessons that can you derive from the experiences of these individuals in building or rebuilding your career.

6. How will you apply the lessons and principles from the lives of these individuals to your career goals?

Day 9

SEEKING GOD FIRST

Like Nehemiah, Joseph was a man who had a clear vision of where he was going and what he was to accomplish in life. But that's not all about him – he actually demonstrated about five distinct qualities that made him to gain mastery in life. These qualities will be of immense help to you as you aim for the top in your career quest and indeed in every other area of your life that you are building or rebuilding. First among the key qualities demonstrated by Joseph was giving God the first place in his life and in everything he did. Expectedly, the results were remarkable.

These exercises will help you to succeed like Joseph:

1. What does it mean to put God first in one's life?

2. Point out three instances in the life of Joseph that proved that God had the first place in his life.

a.

b.

c.

3. Considering how the story of Joseph eventually turned out, did he have any cause to regret submitting himself to the lordship of the Almighty God? YES/NO

4. Give a reason for your answer in exercise 3.

5. Identify, at least, three other persons in the Scripture who defied the odds to give God a priority in their lives.

a.

b.

c.

6. What was the outcome of the decisions of these individuals?

a.

b.

c.

7. Looking at the examples of Joseph and all the others that you have identified, can you honestly say that God has the first place and is in total control of your life? YES/NO/PARTIALLY

8. If your answer to exercise 7 is "NO" or "PARTIALLY", identify the barriers to making God the number one in your life.

9. Aside from prayer, what other personal steps will you take to remove the barriers to your kingdom usefulness?

10. Peter lent his boat to Jesus for soul-winning. What was the result?

11. Identify at least five ways in which you can make yourself useful in the advancement of God's Kingdom.

a.

b.

c.

d.

e.

Day 10

FAVOR FACTOR

"And I said unto the king, If it please the king, and if thy servant have found favour in thy sight, that thou wouldest send me unto Judah, unto the city of my fathers' sepulchres, that I may build it." (Nehemiah 2:5)

Both Nehemiah and Joseph obtained favor – divine and human – and that made a big difference in their lives. In fact, this was one thing that prevented them from being frustrated out of their destiny quests. Despite all that they went through, they had God on their side – and this made it easy for them to find favor in the sight of men who were to be strategic to the fulfillment of their missions.

Take a plunge into the favor fountain with these exercises:

1. Both Nehemiah and Joseph obtained divine favor – but there was also something common to both men that made it easy for them to be God's favor candidates – what was this secret? (See Psalms 102:13 for a clue).

2. Identify specific ways in which you can you apply this secret to your life.

3. When God's favor is released upon you, it does not matter how much you have lost or suffered, a mighty turnaround will happen to you. The Scripture confirms this and even says you will be called a new name. Can you identify what this name is and in what Scripture reference it can be found?

4. Identify the various areas of your life in which you need divine favor and the results you expect to see.

a.

b.

c.

5. Write a prayer request here, listing names of individuals you want God to influence to favor you.

PRAYER REQUEST

Dear Lord, I believe it was you who influenced King Artaxerxes to grant favor to Nehemiah. I know your power remains the same today and forever. For this reason, I ask you to touch the heart of ____to work in my favor. Let every negative feeling toward me be silenced in Jesus' name.

Day 11

POWER OF DILIGENCE

"So built we the wall; and all the wall was joined together unto the half thereof: for the people had a mind to work." (Nehemiah 4:6)

It is one thing to be favored by God, but it is quite another to make that favor continually work for you. This is where diligence comes in. In the realm of champions and achievers, favor brings you in but it is diligence that keeps you in. This we find in the lives of Nehemiah and Joseph. While both men obtained the favor of God and men, they also remained diligent in all they did. In other words, they did not take the grace or favor of God for granted. Similarly, for us to excel in any chosen career, the force of diligence must dominate our being completely.

Discover the power of diligence with these exercises:

1. List, at least, five areas in which in Nehemiah and Joseph demonstrated diligence.

a.

b.

c.

d.

e.

3. Think of ways you can you apply the above principles to your life, especially in building or rebuilding your career. List them below.

4. Identify other areas of your life in which you think the force of diligence is lacking.

5. One way to remedy lack of diligence in any area of life is to deal with time-killers. Identify activities and individuals that drain your time.

Activities	**Individuals**

6. Tackling time-killers and nurturing diligence require having accountability mechanisms in place, so that you can justify what you do with every minute of each day. Think of possible accountability mechanisms that can make you more productive and list them below. The first one is done for you.

- Have a to-do list for each day, carefully listing entries in order of importance.

a.

b.

c.

d.

e.

Day 12

POWER OF PERSEVERANCE

"So we laboured in the work: and half of them held the spears from the rising of the morning till the stars appeared. Likewise at the same time said I unto the people, Let everyone with his servant lodge within Jerusalem, that in the night they may be a guard to us, and labour on the day." (Nehemiah 4:21-22)

The popular saying is true: "Rome was not built in a day." As we find in the experiences of Nehemiah and Joseph, nothing good and enduring is achieved easily or overnight. It takes a lot of patience and endurance. The same goes for any successful career. Building or rebuilding a worthwhile career requires a boatload of patience, and patience must have its perfect work for anything to materialize. Essentially, while favor positions you for success in your quest and diligence keeps you in, it is perseverance that gets you focused on the end result till you achieve it.

Pass the perseverance test with these exercises:

1. How would you define perseverance?

2. Would you describe yourself as possessing this quality?

3. Identify instances in the lives of Joseph that showed that perseverance was a key factor in their accomplishments.

Joseph	**Nehemiah**

4. What can you learn from the above instances and how can you apply them in building your career?

Lesson	**Personal Application**

5. The time of perseverance is indeed a time of great benefit, even though it may not seem immediately obvious to us. In fact, a passage of the Bible encourages us to be joyful for such a moment. Can you identify this Bible passage? What reason does it give for us to be joyful?

Bible Passage	**Reason to be Joyful**

Day 13

POWER OF PRAYER

"And it came to pass, when I heard these words, that I sat down and wept, and mourned certain days, and fasted, and prayed before the God of heaven," (Nehemiah 1:4)

Nehemiah was certainly a man of prayer. This was why prayer came as a natural activity for him as soon as he got the distressing report about Jerusalem and its inhabitants. Evidence abounds of the prayer life of Joseph as well, for as we find in the case of Daniel, being able to interpret a complex dream as that which Joseph interpreted for Pharaoh, requires being in tune with the Spirit of God at all times. These men enjoyed the power that prayer brings and the wonders it produces – as the success of their visions proved. You need prayer to succeed, even in your career.

Take these exercises to explore the power of prayer:

1. What does prayer mean to you?

2. What is the place of prayer in your career dream?

3. God responded to Nehemiah every time, not because he was a special guy, but because he prayed God's word every time. Identify specific promises of God concerning your career that you can take to Him in prayer.

4. For prayer to be effective, certain "prayer-blockers" must be avoided – one of which starts with the letter "u". Can you identify it? (See Matthew 17:20 for a clue).

5. Cultivating and maintaining a habit of prayer, despite the distractions and hustle-bustle of modern life, takes lots of determination and discipline. Write below a daily prayer schedule and steps you'll take to ensure you keep to it.

Day	**Time**
Sunday	
Monday	
Tuesday	
Wednesday	
Thursday	
Friday	
Saturday	

6. Steps I'll take to keep to my prayer schedule

a.

b.

c.

d.

e.

Day 14

BUILDING OR REBUILDING A RELATIONSHIP

"Then I told them of the hand of my God which was good upon me; as also the king's words that he had spoken unto me. And they said, Let us rise up and build. So they strengthened their hands for this good work." (Nehemiah 2:18)

Every relationship, like the wall of Jerusalem, requires a building process – whether it's a new, old or broken one. For a marital relationship, which can be rightly described as the epitome of all human relationships, careful attention must be given to every stage of the building because once there is a breach somewhere, so many things can go wrong later on.

Whether you want to build, rebuild or fix your relationship, the following exercises will help:

1. Identify at least four factors that help in building or rebuilding a successful marital relationship.

a.

b.

c.

d.

e.

2. The confidence of Nehemiah and his companions towards the rebuilding was predicated on two things, according to his testimony in Nehemiah 2:18. What are these?

a.

b.

3. The absence of God in a relationship is best described as building a house on________?

4.List out the five blessings that must be in operation for a marital relationship to be functional.

a.

b.

c.

d.

e.

5. Deuteronomy 28:1,12 tells us that if we_________________ _____________________then all we need to build or rebuild is available at our fingertips.

Day 15

WISDOM

"And I arose in the night, I and some few men with me; neither told I any man what my God had put in my heart to do at Jerusalem: neither was there any beast with me, save the beast that I rode upon." (Nehemiah 2:12)

Wisdom occupied a dominant place in Nehemiah's efforts to rebuild the broken wall of Jerusalem. Without this critical trait, he certainly would have exposed himself, his mission and his companions to needless danger. Many relationships collapse daily, simply because this essential ingredient is lacking.

Master the art of building your relationship with wisdom with the following exercises:

1. What do you understand by "wisdom"?

2. Why is wisdom necessary in building a marriage?

3. Where does true wisdom come from? (Cite two Scripture references to support your answer).

4. One reason that wisdom is so indispensable in our lives is that it comes with a bumper package of seven pillars (Proverbs 9:1) which particularly help to strengthen and stabilize relationships. Itemize these pillars below:

a.

b.

c.

d.

e.

f.

g.

5. A verse in the book of Proverbs reveals to us that even God needed wisdom in building the earth. Where exactly in Proverbs is this?

6. Quote the entire verse in Proverbs (in exercise 5) below:

Day 16

POWER OF LOVE

"That Hanani, one of my brethren, came, he and certain men of Judah; and I asked them concerning the Jews that had escaped, which were left of the captivity, and concerning Jerusalem." (Nehemiah 1:2)

As the example of Jacob, while working for Laban to get his daughter, Rachel, can prove – when we are immersed in love, we are always ready to go the extra mile, regardless of personal inconveniences (Genesis 29:20). The story of Nehemiah's exploit in rebuilding the wall of Jerusalem can never be complete without reference to the driving force of love. It was obviously selfless love that made him inquire of Hanani concerning the condition of the remnant of his people in Jerusalem. That became the foundation of all he did. Nothing works like love in building or rebuilding a relationship.

Experience the power of love as you try the following exercises:

1. What does love mean to you?

2. Look up the meanings of the words “love” and “lust”. How do you think true love is different from lust?

3. True love, like wisdom, has a number of attributes that make it genuine and effective. Outline these 12 attributes as contained in 1 Corinthians 13:4-8.

a.

b.

c.

d.

e.

f.

g.

h.

i.

j.

k

l.

4. How will you make these attributes work in building or rebuilding your relationship? Write your resolves below:

Love Attribute	My Decision
a.	
b.	
c.	
d.	
e.	
f.	
g.	
h.	
i.	
j.	
k	
l.	

Day 17

THE POWER OF FORGIVENESS

"Let thine ear now be attentive, and thine eyes open, that thou mayest hear the prayer of thy servant, which I pray before thee now, day and night, for the children of Israel thy servants, and confess the sins of the children of Israel, which we have sinned against thee: both I and my father's house have sinned." (Nehemiah 1:6)

Forgiveness is a powerful tool in building or rebuilding a relationship. In fact, it is the indispensable wheel on which relationships survive. Due to issues bordering on misunderstanding and individual differences, offenses must come in every human relationship. So, every relationship that will endure the test of time must consist of individuals who are perpetual forgivers. However, that we must perpetually forgive gives no one the license to perpetually offend. Not only that, for forgiveness to be effective and for a relationship to be healed, there must be sincere confession of faults and considerate communication of feelings. We find this in the case of Nehemiah. He sincerely acknowledged that it was the Israelites' sin that brought ruin to them; he therefore sought forgiveness from God with a penitent heart.

Transform your relationship with the power of forgiveness with these exercises:

1. In what areas have you offended your partner for which you must seek forgiveness?

2. Are there offenses you are holding on to and struggling to let go?

3. Outline steps you will take to let go of the weight of offenses.

4. Why does the Scripture counsel against allowing the sun to go down on our wrath according to Ephesians 4:26-27?

5. To ensure true forgiveness and sincere reconciliation, ___________must not precede confession.

6. A way to minimize offenses is to pay good attention to your partner's likes and dislikes. Make a list of your partner's likes and dislikes below (gestures they appreciate and those they are uncomfortable with)

My Partner's Likes	**My Partner's Dislikes**

7. Now that you have a good view of your partner's likes and dislikes, itemize ways you can improve relationship between the two of you below:

a.

b.

c.

d.

e.

Day 18

UNITED PRAYER

"Then said I unto them, Ye see the distress that we are in, how Jerusalem lieth waste, and the gates thereof are burned with fire: come, and let us build up the wall of Jerusalem, that we be no more a reproach." (Nehemiah 2:17)

Things are looking good, aren't they? After you and your partner have opened up to each other in sincere confession and forgiveness, then it is time to pray for your relationship to be healed. There is immeasurable power in unity of purpose. This was why Nehemiah sought the cooperation of those within his circle of influence to join him in rebuilding the wall of Jerusalem. It is particularly interesting that despite the fact that the wall had been in ruins for, at least, twenty years, Nehemiah was confident that with collective effort, it could be rebuilt. This is the same approach with which the Lord expects you and your partner to approach the task of praying for your relationship – no matter how bad things have been.

Take the following exercises to savor the blessing of united prayer:

1. There is boundless power in united prayer. Can you point out at least four instances in the Scripture where the power of collective prayer is mentioned?

a.

b.

c.

d.

2. Mention at least four instances in the Scripture where the power of collective prayer is demonstrated.

a.

b.

c.

d.

3. Philippians 4:6-7 tells us the right approach to prayer. How do you think the principles outlined in the verse can be applied to praying for your relationship?

4. Create a prayer schedule for you and your partner.

Day	**Time**
Monday	
Today	
Wednesday	

5. Identify factors that can prevent this schedule from working out and the steps you will take to manage them.

Possible barrier	**Steps I will take**
a.	
b.	
c.	
d.	

Day 19

POWER OF FASTING

"And it came to pass, when I heard these words, that I sat down and wept, and mourned certain days, and fasted, and prayed before the God of heaven," (Nehemiah 1:4)

Nehemiah used a combination of the different principles previously discussed to get the rebuilding project started. He applied wisdom in approaching the king and the people (wisdom); he loved the people enough not to leave the city of Jerusalem in ruins (love); he asked God for forgiveness of all their sins (forgiveness); and he wept and mourned in united prayer with the people for the healing of their land (united prayer). But he went beyond all these to also apply the principle of fasting, which, when done right, as in his case, has been known to bring down the invincible power of God.

Explore the power of fasting with these exercises:

1. Fasting is sometimes necessary for prayer to be effective. Can you find a Scripture reference for this?

2. Fasting is not just about going hungry but rather a time to _______________, and _____________________

3. Make a list of 5 people or groups of people in the Bible who engaged in fasting and the result they got.

a.

b.

c.

d.

e.

4. Isaiah 58 provides a picture of the kind of fast acceptable to God. Can you mention five characteristics of this fast?

a.

b.

c.

d.

e.

5. Try fasting; it works wonders. With consideration for the state of your health, make a monthly fasting routine for yourself below, devoting each fasting day to a request.

	Day	Time (From __to___)
Week 1		
Week 2		
Week 3		
Week 4		

Day 20

BUILDING OR REBUILDING A FAMILY

"And they said unto me, The remnant that are left of the captivity there in the province are in great affliction and reproach: the wall of Jerusalem also is broken down, and the gates thereof are burned with fire." (Nehemiah 1:3)

Nehemiah realized that the family unit in Jerusalem had disintegrated completely and, as a result, the wall was completely broken down. Today in our society, the same is true and the result is a broken down society and massive incarceration among the youths, especially among the minorities and single parents. As such, like Nehemiah, we must be determined to build or rebuild areas of our lives in ruins and to reinforce areas that are doing well. These include our families.

Take the following exercises on family building and rebuilding:

1. Identify two reasons we must build and guard our families, according to Exodus 23:26 and Psalms 127:3-5.

a.

b.

2. Why is the devil particularly interested in destroying the family unit?

3. It is the will of God that every member of our household serves the Lord. Can you cite a passage of the Scripture for this promise?

4. Take a critical look at your family to see if this will of God is being fulfilled in each member.

5. Itemize below steps you will take to build/rebuild and guard your family. One has been done for you:

a. Attend a seminar on building a godly family

b.

c.

d.

e.

Day 21

STABLE HOMES

"Then Eliashib the high priest rose up with his brethren the priests, and they builded the sheep gate; they sanctified it, and set up the doors of it; even unto the tower of Meah they sanctified it, unto the tower of Hananeel." (Nehemiah 3:1)

Having a stable home, where children could be safely raised, is of great importance. Take a look at the first family - when their home became unstable, every other thing fell apart. When they were evicted from the Garden of Eden, due to the fault of the parents, the home environment became unhealthy to raise children in. Of the two children they had, one was murdered and the other became a vagabond and a fugitive. This is why the need for a stable home to give our children the best opportunity to thrive is very important.

Try the following exercises on building a stable home.

1. Building a stable home takes personal decision and determination. Two men in the Old Testaments made such a personal decision. Can you mention their names and the relevant Scripture references

where they made their decisions? (Clue: One is a prophet with a name starting with letter "I").

2. Being a godly parent is not an automatic guarantee of a godly family or stable home. Identify at least three parents in the Bible who were godly but had unruly children.

a.

b.

c.

3. Can you pinpoint where each of the parents above missed it?

Parent	Parenting Fault
a.	
b.	
c.	

4. What steps will you take to avoid the errors of the parents identified in the above exercise?

Parenting Fault	Steps to Avoid it

5. A family expert has identified the following characteristics of a godly and stable family. Write **yes** or **no** after each as applicable to your family:

- **Joy is characteristic of a godly/stable home.** Every marriage and every family will experience trials and hardships of various kinds, but there is no circumstance that can rob us of our joy if we know that the key to our present welfare and future destiny lies in Christ alone.
- **A godly/stable home is orderly.** The members of the household regularly review everything that's allowed in. Should it stay? Does it build up the family? Does it encourage people to value one another over things?
- **A godly/stable home is marked by grace.** It is a retreat where the hurting can find comfort, rest and healing.
- **A godly/stable home is a place of service.** Its atmosphere is tempered and flavored with acts of kindness, respect, humility, and love.
- **A godly/stable home is a place where the spiritual disciplines are practiced.** It provides an environment where every member of the family learns how to live by studying the Scriptures, praying, meditating on God's Word, and spending time alone and together in the presence of the Lord.
- **A godly/stable home is based on God's purposes for every member of the household.** It's a place where the family's goals are founded upon His values and where the corporate vision of the future is consistent with His plan.

6. If you have written NO for any of the above, write down the steps you will take to set things right in your home henceforth.

a.

b.

c.

Day 22

BUILDING GODLY CHARACTER

"And I arose in the night, I and some few men with me; neither told I any man what my God had put in my heart to do at Jerusalem: neither was there any beast with me, save the beast that I rode upon." (Nehemiah 2:12)

Nehemiah was, from all indications, a man of impeccable and exemplary character. He was a man of integrity whose conduct and reputation have earned him the trust and respect of the people around him over the years. Thus, despite the fact that he had not revealed his intentions on why he was returning to Jerusalem, few men of high repute followed him and were willing to risk even their own lives. This is what developing and maintaining a godly character can achieve in your life, family and general endeavors.

Take the following exercises on cultivating godly character:

1. What does it mean to have a "godly character"?

2. Can you identify, at least nine character traits of God as revealed in the Scripture?

a.

b.

c.

d.

e.

f.

g.

h.

i.

3. How can you emulate and replicate each of the above traits as a parent in your household?

	Character trait	My resolve
a.		
b.		
c.		
d.		
e.		
f.		
g.		

h.

i.

	God's character trait	**My decision as a parent**
a.		
b.		
c.		
d.		
e.		
f.		
g.		
h.		
i.		

4. Is there any particular godly character trait that you particularly struggle with as a parent? YES/NO

5. If yes to the above, which is it, and what step will you take to develop it?

Day 23

GODLY TRAINING

"They which builded on the wall, and they that bare burdens, with those that laded, everyone with one of his hands wrought in the work, and with the other hand held a weapon." (Nehemiah 4:17)

When God invented a family system, He also designed an instructional manual to help educate and train so that we can be fulfilled. Nehemiah's men were trained and seasoned warriors; they worked with one hand and held a weapon in the other. Without proper training, the rebuilding effort would have been greatly hampered. Similarly, a family is an organization that requires constant training, and the instruction from the Scripture is to begin the training while our children are young, and to continue so that they will not depart from the way of the Lord.

Take the following exercises to evaluate your training efforts:

1. Identify four parents in the Scripture who evidently gave godly training to their children.

a.

b.

c.

d.

2. State vital lessons you can learn from the parenting style of each of the parents above.

Parent	Lesson

a.

b.

c.

d.

3. Point out three Scripture references in Proverbs where God specifically asks parents to train/instruct/discipline their children.

a.

b.

c.

4. Which of the above Scriptural injunctions are you not fully complying with?

5. What steps will you take to remedy the above area of non-compliance?

Day 24

GODLY DISCIPLINE

"But if ye turn unto me, and keep my commandments, and do them; though there were of you cast out unto the uttermost part of the heaven, yet will I gather them from thence, and will bring them unto the place that I have chosen to set my name there." (Nehemiah 1:9)

Nehemiah realized that godly sorrow leads to repentance, so he reminded God of His promise that if the children of Israel sinned and were divinely chastised, upon their repentance, God would be merciful and restore them back to their rightful place. No parent wants to needlessly rebuke or disengage from their children, but when a child misbehaves, it becomes the duty of a godly parent to discipline and correct.

Explore the principles of godly discipline with these exercises:

1. What do you understand by godly discipline?

2. God is a loving God; yet He takes discipline of His people seriously. Can you point out three Scripture references where God disciplined His children?

a.

b.

c.

3. Who was/were disciplined in each of the references and what was the reason?

	Who	**Reason**
a.		
b.		
c.		

4. Just as He is a "disciplinarian", God equally instructs us as parents to discipline our children. Point out three references where discipline for our children is instructed?

a.

b.

c.

5. Where there is no discipline, lots of things go wrong with the children and the entire family. Identify three families in the Scripture in which discipline of children was neglected and the consequences.

Family	Consequence
a.	
b.	
c.	

6. __________should be the overriding principle in disciplining our children.

7. Why should parents not allow anger take over their emotions when disciplining their children?

Day 25

PRAYER AS THE MASTER KEY

"O Lord, I beseech thee, let now thine ear be attentive to the prayer of thy servant, and to the prayer of thy servants, who desire to fear thy name: and prosper, I pray thee, thy servant this day, and grant him mercy in the sight of this man. For I was the king's cupbearer." (Nehemiah 1:11)

Nehemiah prayed all manner of prayers—for repentance, for favor with the king and the people, for his adversaries, for unity of the people after the wall was completed, and so on. This is in line with the expectation of God that we pray all kinds of prayer. One essential prayer activity we must engage in is praying for our children to mold their lives and safeguard their destinies. In the Gospels, Jesus rebuked His disciples for not allowing parents to bring their children closer to Him. We can infer from this that it is the duty of parents to bring their children to Jesus in prayer, and every time they do so, they are asking Jesus to lay His hand upon them.

Try the following exercises to strengthen your prayer for your children:

1. Identify three reasons why you should make prayer a key element in training your children.

a.

b.

c.

2. Prayer that will be effective for our children must be based on:

3. Outline at least 10 prayer requests you can make on behalf of your children, based on God's promises as revealed in the Scriptures.

a.

b.

c.

d.

e.

f.

g.

g.

h.

i.

4. Prepare a prayer schedule for each of your children. (While you pray for them all generally on a daily basis, you can choose a specific day of the week for each of them to present their particular needs to God.)

Day	Child's name

Day 26

BUILDING OR REBUILDING A BUSINESS

"And I went out by night by the gate of the valley, even before the dragon well, and to the dung port, and viewed the walls of Jerusalem, which were broken down, and the gates thereof were consumed with fire." (Nehemiah 2:13)

As we have applied Nehemiah's principles and strategies in rebuilding the wall of Jerusalem to various aspects of our lives, we can also apply it to building or rebuilding very successful business enterprises. As the second chapter of his book tells us, Nehemiah went out by night by the gate of the valley, even before the dragon well. What an adventure! To build or rebuild thriving businesses will require us to pull some late nights, going over ideas and strategies, encountering obstacles and difficulties and scaling them.

Take the following exercises as you do some business exploits with Nehemiah's tactics:

1. In building or rebuilding a successful business, we must pay careful attention to the f__ ___ ___ ___ ___ ___ ___ ___ __

2. Why should you make Christ the very foundation of even your business endeavors?

3. The example of________________in the Scripture shows us that it is not enough to make Christ the foundation of our businesses – we must partner with and involve Him all the way.

4. Itemize ways in which you can demonstrate that Christ is your foundation and partner in business

a.

b.

c.

d.

e

5. Outline ways in which you will henceforth make your business help in advancing God's Kingdom

a.

b.

c.

d.

e.

Day 27

BUILDING INTEGRITY

"Moreover I said unto the king, If it please the king, let letters be given me to the governors beyond the river, that they may convey me over till I come into Judah;" (Nehemiah 2:7)

Any business that will stand the test of time must have the hallmark of integrity. There is no doubt that Nehemiah was a man of impeccable integrity who had served the king for at least twenty years as the cupbearer. Nehemiah had never had a sad countenance before the king. He probably had never 'called in sick' since he started working in the palace; so when he came in with a sad countenance, the king was quick to ask the cause. He made his request known to the king and it was granted without any reservations—the power of integrity!

Take the following exercises to position yourself for the blessings of integrity upon your business:

1. What should be your major focus in building or rebuilding a business?

2. List five benefits of integrity to building or rebuilding a business.

a.

b.

c.

d.

e.

3. Using 1 Timothy 3:1-9 as a base, itemize at least six qualities that show integrity in a business builder or rebuilder.

a.

b.

c,

d,

e.

f.

4. In what areas have you fallen short of demonstrating integrity in the past?

5. What steps will you take from now on to make integrity your watchword?

a.

b.

c.

Day 28

DEVELOPING KNOWLEDGE OF WITTY INVENTIONS AND WISE PLANNING

"Then the king said unto me, For what dost thou make request? So I prayed to the God of heaven. And I said unto the king, If it please the king, and if thy servant have found favour in thy sight, that thou wouldest send me unto Judah, unto the city of my fathers' sepulchres, that I may build it. And the king said unto me, (the queen also sitting by him,) For how long shall thy journey be? and when wilt thou return? So it pleased the king to send me; and I set him a time." (Nehemiah 2:4-6)

It took Nehemiah about six months before he acted on the information given to him by Hanani - from the month of Chisleu to the month of Nisan. This is a demonstration of wisdom. It requires a great deal of wise planning and a God-given idea to build or rebuild anything. Moreover, when the king asked him for his request, he wasted no time in answering him, which not only encouraged the king to grant his request but also saved him from severe punishment. Developing wittiness and wise planning is not only required to build or rebuild, but lacking it could simply mean that your business idea is dead on arrival.

The following exercises will enhance your knowledge of witty inventions:

1. Where does knowledge of witty inventions come from, according to Proverbs 8:12?

2. What principally distinguishes the business of a believer in Christ from a non-believer?

3. There are many secrets of business success that only God reveal. Cite a Scripture reference that shows that God is a custodian of secrets.

4. Why must every Christian man or woman be filled with the Holy Spirit?

5. Are you filled with the Holy Spirit? YES/NO

6. If your answer to exercise 5 is NO, make a decision to be filled within the next three days.

7. If your answer to exercise 5 is YES, how often do you engage the Holy Spirit in your business-building plan? EVERY TIME/ SOMETIMES/NOT SURE

8. If your answer to the above is SOMETIMES or NOT SURE. Resolve to make engagement of the Holy Spirit in your business a daily affair. Write your decision below.

I______________________(your name) will daily engage the Holy Spirit in all my business activities.

Day 29

TREATING PEOPLE RIGHT

"Then said I unto them, Ye see the distress that we are in, how Jerusalem lieth waste, and the gates thereof are burned with fire: come, and let us build up the wall of Jerusalem, that we be no more a reproach. Then I told them of the hand of my God which was good upon me; as also the king's words that he had spoken unto me. And they said, Let us rise up and build. So they strengthened their hands for this good work." (Nehemiah 2:17-18)

Businesses thrive on good relationships with all those who are connected to it – employees, customers, suppliers, investors and so on. Even in the land of captivity, Nehemiah obviously had everything going well for him--which honestly suggests that the care of the people back in Jerusalem should be less of his concern--but not this guy. He wanted to be treated like his people, which explains why he later became the governor of his people. He treated his people with respect. You must treat people right to succeed in business.

Take the following exercises to boost your people skills:

1. What do you understand by treating people right as a business builder or rebuilder?

2. Jesus gave us a universal and timeless principle on relating with others with consideration. Where in the Scripture can this be found?

3. List out specific ways in which you can treat the following people right:

Your employees

Your customers

Your investors

4. Mention two individuals in the Scripture who demonstrated wrong business ethics in dealing with others.

a.

b.

5. What lessons can you personally derive from the shortcomings of the above people?

6. In what ways have you fallen short in your treatment of people connected to your business in the past?

7. What will you differently from now on?

Day 30

FAITHFULNESS IN FINANCIAL MATTERS WITH GOD

"And a letter unto Asaph the keeper of the king's forest, that he may give me timber to make beams for the gates of the palace which appertained to the house, and for the wall of the city, and for the house that I shall enter into. And the king granted me, according to the good hand of my God upon me. Then I came to the governors beyond the river, and gave them the king's letters. Now the king had sent captains of the army and horsemen with me." (Nehemiah 2:8-9)

While we have no record of Nehemiah's financial dealings with King Artaxerxes, evidence reveals that he was a well-trusted aide, despite occupying a very sensitive position. He must have proved himself faithful over the years to make the king entrust his very life to him. God is looking for such faithful ambassadors like Nehemiah today, especially in the area of financial matters.

Take the following exercises on financial accountability to God:

1. Honoring God with our finances and other resources is not only a way of demonstrating faithfulness but actually obedience to a scriptural command and a way to accessing unlimited blessings. Where in the Bible can this truth be found?

2. Identify six "substances" you can honor God with:

a.

b.

c.

d.

e.

f.

3. Mention specific ways in which you can honor God with the above substances.

	Substance	Way to honor God
a.		
b.		
c.		
d.		
e.		
f.		

4. Have you been faithful in the above-listed ways of honoring God? YES/NO/SOMETIMES.

5. If your answer to the above is NO or SOMETIMES, itemize things you will do differently from now on to improve your financial accountability to God and open the door of blessing upon your business.

a.

b.

c.

d.

6. What do you understand by tithing? How is it different from offering?

7.What benefits, according to the Scripture, do faithful tithers enjoy?

Day 31

THE POWER OF CONTINUOUS TRAINING AND IMPROVEMENT

"In what place therefore ye hear the sound of the trumpet, resort ye thither unto us: our God shall fight for us. So we laboured in the work: and half of them held the spears from the rising of the morning till the stars appeared." (Nehemiah 4:20-21)

Nehemiah, as strategic builder, devoted time to training and motivating his team. He was obviously a man that believed in process, as it became quite obvious in his training style and technique. There were clear instructions on hand on how to respond when the people heard the sound of the trumpet, where to gather, and what to do there. He addressed the how, when, where and what, which are the essential elements of a good training and improvement protocol. This significantly helped to boost the morale of his companions, as well as prepping them for best performance. You can learn a lot from him in building or rebuilding your business enterprise.

Take the following exercises to demonstrate lessons from Nehemiah's success:

1. Proverbs 24:3-4 reveals three key elements that must be carefully considered for a business to succeed. What are these?

a.

b.

c.

2. Paul was comparatively a more successful apostle than Peter, despite being a "newcomer". Itemize the attributes in him that accounted for his exceptional achievements.

3. How can you apply the principles from the lives of Nehemiah and Paul to enhance your business success?

Lesson from Nehemiah	**How I will apply it to my business**
a.	
b.	
c.	

Lesson from Paul	**How I will apply it to my business**
a.	
b.	
c.	

4. Apart from Nehemiah and Paul, can you mention, at least, three others in the Scripture who enjoyed outstanding success due to continuous self-development?

a.

b.

c.

5. How will you apply lessons from the lives of these people to your business?

Day 32

THE BONDAGE BREAKER

"And our adversaries said, They shall not know, neither see, till we come in the midst among them, and slay them, and cause the work to cease." (Nehemiah 4:11)

Nehemiah had some formidable adversaries, who were bent on frustrating his efforts and making him a failure. Compared to modern times, these adversaries can be likened to addictions—whose only purpose is to destroy their host. Nehemiah's adversaries said, "They shall not know, neither see till we come in the midst among them, and slay them, and cause the work to cease." This exactly is how addictions operate. The good news, however, is that God is able to deliver anyone from any form of addiction, no matter how strong it may be.

Take the following exercises to discover the power of the bondage-breaker.

1. Addictions may take many forms and shapes – but they all originate from only one source. Can you identify the influencer and encourager of these yokes?

2. Point out at least three examples from the Scripture to illustrate your answer in exercise one.

a.

b.

c.

3. Addictions have a source, but there is also a process through which they enslave their victims. Using Matthew 13:25, can you identify this?

4. Knowing the different routes through which addictions penetrate the lives of individuals is one sure way to prevent them. Outline three ways through which one can get entangled in the yoke of addiction.

a.

b.

c.

5. Who possesses the power to break the chains of addiction, according to 1 John 3:8?

Day 33

THE EFFECT OF SOCIALIZATION

"The words of Nehemiah the son of Hachaliah. And it came to pass in the month Chisleu, in the twentieth year, as I was in Shushan the palace" (Nehemiah 1:1)

Addiction, for many, often begins with socialization. It begins when we choose to acquire a personal identity and learn the norms, values, behaviors and social skills that are completely contrary to the word of God. Nehemiah had lived in captivity for at least twenty years as at the time the report of the condition of the wall of Jerusalem was given to him. He had lived in the palace and had both influence and affluence. Being the king's cupbearer meant that he was highly influential, yet he refused to imbibe the identity and norms, values and behaviors of the Persian people who were idolaters. In effect, he was able to conquer one of the most powerful routes through which addiction penetrates the life of an individual.

Take the following exercises to discover power over socialization-induced addiction:

1. What do you understand by socialization?

2. Addiction through socialization comes through four major avenues. Can you identify these?

a.

b.

c.

d.

3. Briefly describe what each of the above routes entails

Route	Description
a.	
b.	
c.	
d.	
e.	

4. How can you apply your understanding of these various routes of addiction through socialization to prevent becoming a victim yourself?

Route of Addiction	Description	Personal Application

6. A powerful exhortation, which is equally an effective antidote to addiction, is contained in the book of Romans. Can you identify the chapter and verse?

7. Take a scrutiny of your life. Can you identify any particular addiction? If yes, what is it?

8. Following the principles you have discovered so far about victory over addiction and your understanding of the power of Christ to break the chain of addiction, outline the steps you will take within the next few days to obtain total freedom.

a.

b.

c.

Day 34

THE PROBLEM WITH BAD COMPANY

"But when Sanballat the Horonite, and Tobiah the servant, the Ammonite, and Geshem the Arabian, heard it, they laughed us to scorn, and despised us, and said, What is this thing that ye do? will ye rebel against the king?" (Nehemiah 2:19)

Nehemiah was smart enough to know that evil communication can corrupt the best of manners. Sanballat, Tobiah and Geshem are names synonymous with evil—and Nehemiah wasted no time in steering clear of them. Like all destroyers and addictions, the men did all they could to entice him; they invited him many times to come and associate with them, but knowing that their real intention was to stop the progress of the work, he denied their invitation every time.

Take the exercises below to discover further principles of overcoming the snare of bad company:

1. There are three factors that determine whether one falls into enslavement of bad company or not. Identify the factors below.

a.

b.

c.

2. Briefly explain how these factors work

a.

b.

c.

3. Knowing the destructive influence that the wrong company can have on the best of individuals, the Scripture strictly warns against intimate relationship with the ungodly. Can you point out four of such warnings? (Make it two in the Old Testament and two in the New).

a.

b.

c.

d.

4. Sincerely consider those you regard as your close companions. Is there any that is not having a very good influence on you? YES/NO.

5. If your answer to the above exercise is YES, what steps will you take in the course of the next few weeks to untangle yourself from such? Write down your resolutions.

a.

b.

c.

Day 35

TIME TO EVERY PURPOSE

"And the king said unto me, (the queen also sitting by him,) For how long shall thy journey be? and when wilt thou return? So it pleased the king to send me; and I set him a time." (Nehemiah 2:6)

Time-consciousness is certainly one of the strong points of Nehemiah and is indeed a major attribute of most conquerors and achievers in life. The king asked Nehemiah the duration of his journey and his anticipated time of return. As simple as these questions sound, they are lifesavers. If you are careful with your time, you will not lose in life. I firmly believe that a life of addiction begins with poor time management, because if you spend your time in a wrong place with the wrong kind of people, the result will be bad!

Take the following exercises to maximize the power of time-management:

1. As Ecclesiastes 3:1 reveals, a life that must avoid addiction must be a life that has found its_____________________

2. There is a purpose for your life – the reason for which you were born into the world. Have you discovered this?

3. If your answer to exercise 2 is YES, write down the steps you are taking or that you will take henceforth to prevent yourself from being derailed by poor time management and modern day distractions.

a.

b.

c.

d.

e.

4. If your answer to exercise 2 is NO, take the following steps for a clue to your purpose:

- Take time to ask God in prayer His purpose for sending you into the world.
- Look within to discover your passion.
- Consider an activity that you do very easily, while others struggle.
- Think of that activity that people often commend you for and think you do exceptionally.

5. Social media has become like a hurricane, sweeping away people's time, together with their commitment to their purpose. Sincerely ask yourself:

- How much time do I spend on the social media daily?
- Do the activities I engage in on social media edify me in every way?
- Do I become restless when I have not checked my social media accounts in a day?
- Is social media distracting my attention from the things of God and other important aspects of my life?
- Do I depend on social media for validation – and are social media comments beginning to influence my moods, actions and attitudes?

You sincere answers to these questions will let you know whether you are becoming a casualty of the forces of the last days or not.

6. If you think you are being derailed from your purpose through social media, outline the steps you will take henceforth to get back on track.

a.

b.

c.

d.

e.

Day 36

BEING ACCOUNTABLE

"Moreover I said unto the king, If it please the king, let letters be given me to the governors beyond the river, that they may convey me over till I come into Judah; And a letter unto Asaph the keeper of the king's forest, that he may give me timber to make beams for the gates of the palace which pertained to the house, and for the wall of the city, and for the house that I shall enter into. And the king granted me, according to the good hand of my God upon me." (Nehemiah 2:7-8)

Accountability is a proven defense against addiction and other thieves of time, purpose and destiny. In the case of Nehemiah, he was very much ready to rebuild wall of Jerusalem, the moment Hanani informed him about the situation of the remnant in the city. However, he had to request from the king a letter to be given to him so that he might obtain the needed materials for rebuilding the wall. Nehemiah was, from that moment, accountable to the king regarding his time, the supplies and the people back in Jerusalem. His sense of accountability to the king kept his focus on his mission and not allowing his adversaries to stop the work. The following exercises will help improve your sense of accountability:

1. Briefly explain what it means to be accountable.

2. There are three major causes of loss of a sense of accountability. Can you identify them?

a.

b.

c.

3. What are the big three assets for which we must be accountable?

a.

b.

c.

4. In what ways can you manage your time, the people in your life and your money, so that you remain accountable for them at all times?

Ways to maintain accountability:

- Time

- People

- Money

5. In what ways can good advice keep you from addiction and lack of accountability, according to Proverbs 1:8-9?

6. Who are you accountable to?

7. If, until now, you had no one to whom you are accountable. Outline the steps you will take to make yourself accountable.

a.

b.

c.

Day 37

NEGLECTING EVIL BEHAVIOR

"But it came to pass, that when Sanballat heard that we builded the wall, he was wroth, and took great indignation, and mocked the Jews." (Nehemiah 4:1)

Successfully tackling and completing a task requires facing it head on, without allowing distractions. Same goes for addiction, if it must be overcome, it must not be neglected but decisively dealt with. The devil wants us to focus on the minor so that we neglect the major. This is his number one strategy. Once the devil gets our attention away from our main objective, then he can easily cut us off. Nehemiah was focused on the wall, but his adversaries were more focused on mockery, telling him that the quality of the work performed was substandard.

The following exercises will help you on the path of victory over all that you need to overcome.

1. What exactly does it mean to neglect something?

2. Outline the three ways through which Satan deceives people into neglecting their addictions.

a.

b.

c.

3. An effective way to deal with addiction is to accept the great salvation that Christ offers. Have you been born again? YES/NO

4. If your answer to the above is NO, now is the time to receive Jesus into our heart. Close your eyes and ask the Lord to forgive your sins and make you His child. Invite Jesus into your life to reside permanently. If you pray with sincerity, He will come into your heart and give you power to overcome addiction to any bad habit.

5. Belonging to a fellowship of true believers equally helps. Do you attend a Bible-believing church, where the truth of God's word is preached to give you total victory over the flesh and the world? YES/NO

6. If your answer to exercise 5 is YES, how regularly do you attend? REGULARLY/NOT REGULARLY

7. If your answer to the above is NOT REGULARLY, identify what hinders you from regular church attendance and outline ways you are going to overcome it henceforth.

a.

b.

c.

8. If your answer to exercise 5 is NO, make a decision today to prayerfully identify a living church around you to attend regularly.

Day 38

HEALTH MATTERS

"And they said unto me, The remnant that are left of the captivity there in the province are in great affliction and reproach: the wall of Jerusalem also is broken down, and the gates thereof are burned with fire." (Nehemiah 1:3)

Health issues are very real, more so now that we live in a world of genetically altered, processed and fast foods. The incidence of people getting ill is at an alarming rate and the need to address our health issues is not only necessary but urgent and important. Nehemiah was told about the deplorable condition of the people in Jerusalem; the economy was not in a good shape, relationship with God was non-existent and the health of the people was in chaos. Many relationships, businesses, families and careers have been destroyed because of a major illness; so the need to rebuild after an episode of illness must be addressed with all sincerity.

Take the following exercises to discover how.

1. Identify five principles that can enhance healing and sound health.

a.

b.

c.

d

e.

2. Outline 5 Scripture references in which God promises His children healing and health.

a.

b.

c.

d.

e.

3. It sounds ironical to many that fasting can be helpful to our health. Can you point out a major health benefit of fasting?

4. Is God against visiting hospital or use of medication? Find two Scripture references to explain your answers.

a.

b.

5. Jeremiah 8:22 talks about "balm in Gilead". What/Who is our Balm today?

Day 39

ENEMIES OF PROGRESS

"But when Sanballat the Horonite, and Tobiah the servant, the Ammonite, and Geshem the Arabian, heard it, they laughed us to scorn, and despised us, and said, What is this thing that ye do? will ye rebel against the king?" (Nehemiah 2:19)

There's never a perfect time or scenario to start building or rebuilding; there will always be obstacles, oppositions and discouragement, even when it is the appointed time to arise and build. Nehemiah encountered three difficult personalities—terrible individuals—who were bent on frustrating efforts to rebuild the wall of Jerusalem. These men were Sanballat, Tobiah, and Geshem—men of negative influence! These were the enemies Nehemiah encountered in his days; unfortunately, their likes are still very much around today.

The following exercises will guide you on the path of victory over them.

1. Who was Sanballat, and what does he represent to your current effort to rebuild?

2. How can you fight an enemy you cannot see?

3. Since the battles we fight as believers are mostly spiritual, mention the weapons we can use to overcome as contained in Ephesians 6:10-18

____

____

____

____

____

____

____

4. Write down the place of each of the above weapons to your victory in spiritual warfare.

Weapon **Significance**

Day 40

WHO WAS TOBIAH?

"But it came to pass, that when Sanballat, and Tobiah, and the Arabians, and the Ammonites, and the Ashdodites, heard that the walls of Jerusalem were made up, and that the breaches began to be stopped, then they were very wroth." (Nehemiah 4:7)

Satan does not launch his attacks against us in one way. He tries different approaches and methods. This is why we are encouraged to be sober and vigilant, so as not to be caught unawares. Nehemiah, on his part, took time to study his enemies. He understood their mode of attack, their time of attack, the style of their attack, and the weapon of their attack. In like manner, his enemies took time to study Nehemiah, looking for his moment of weakness, weariness and carelessness. One of such enemies was Tobiah.

Take the following exercises as you trample upon the spirit of Tobiah in your rebuilding effort.

1. What does the spirit of Tobiah represent to your current rebuilding effort?

2. In which particular form does the spirit of Tobiah manifest today to derail people from their destinies?

3. Cite two instances from the Scripture where we are warned to beware of the manifestation of the spirit of Tobiah.

a.

b.

4. Cite an example of the manifestation of the spirit of Tobiah in the Scripture.

5. We need the help of ____________________ to overcome the spirit of Tobiah successfully.

Day 41

WHO WAS GESHEM?

"That Sanballat and Geshem sent unto me, saying, Come, let us meet together in some one of the villages in the plain of Ono. But they thought to do me mischief." (Nehemiah 6:2)

Nehemiah was always battle ready. He never allowed himself to be distracted; rather he kept his eyes on the end result which was to rebuild the broken wall of Jerusalem. Sanballat (enemy in secret) and Tobiah (camouflage) did everything possible to get Nehemiah off the wall; he was bullied, threatened and offered a compromise but he prevailed by his willingness to follow God's plans wholly. Since Sanballat and Tobiah could not prevail against Nehemiah, they brought another weapon to fight him—Geshem. Take the following exercises on your path to victory.

1. What does the spirit of Geshem represent?

2. What is the purpose of the spirit of Geshen?

3. In what ways can the spirit manifest to contend with a believer who is rebuilding today?

4. The Spirit of God through Prophet Isaiah has assured us of victory over the spirit of Geshem. Where in the Scripture can this promise be found?

5. What is the most effective way to overcome the spirit of Geshem, according to 1 Peter 5:9?

Day 42

THE PLAINS OF ONO

"That Sanballat and Geshem sent unto me, saying, Come, let us meet together in some one of the villages in the plain of Ono. But they thought to do me mischief." (Nehemiah 6:2)

Nehemiah was diligent and determined to see the wall of Jerusalem completely rebuilt. There were many adversaries against this mission; those that were bent on stopping the rebuilders from rebuilding the wall. We fight the same enemies today, and their singular mission is to get us to abandon building or rebuilding our lives. Sanballat and Geshem sent a message to Nehemiah to meet them in one of the villages in the plain of Ono. They came five times with the same invitation, but Nehemiah resisted and refused to come down from rebuilding the wall.

Try the following exercises to master the art of concentration like Nehemiah:

1. What two meanings does Ono symbolize and how can they relate to your current rebuilding effort?

Meaning Symbolism Relationship to my rebuilding goal

a.

b..

2. What lesson can you personally learn from the enemies' persistent invitation to Nehemiah to the plains of Ono?

3. How will you apply this lesson to your rebuilding efforts?

4. What six tactics does the enemy use to try to get us to "the plain of Ono"?

a.

b.

c.

d.

e.

f.

Day 43

TACTIC #1: MOCKERY

"But when Sanballat the Horonite, and Tobiah the servant, the Ammonite, and Geshem the Arabian, heard it, they laughed us to scorn, and despised us, and said, What is this thing that ye do? will ye rebel against the king?" (Nehemiah 2:19)

Mockery, teasing, or taunting is one major weapon that Satan uses against anyone making efforts to rebuild their life. The essence is to make the rebuilder lose self-confidence, as well as belief in the rebuilding effort. In the case of Nehemiah, mockery was one of the first weapons of choice used against him. Sanballat, Tobiah and Geshem laughed Nehemiah to scorn and despised him. Sanballat mocked everyone helping Nehemiah; he even called them feeble and called their sincerity to question.

Take the following exercises to see how familiar you are with this tactic of the enemy:

1. Mockery is a common weapon that the enemy uses against all who have a significant purpose to fulfill in life. Can you mention at least two other person in the Scripture whom the enemy used this weapon against?

a.

b.

2. What is the particular goal of the enemy in using the weapon of mockery against builders and rebuilders of destiny?

3. What does the rampant use of the weapon of mockery by the enemy tell you as a person and how should you prepare yourself?

4. Apostle Peter was one of the people inspired by the Holy Spirit to warn us on the pervasiveness of the spirit of mockery in the last days. Where in his epistles can this warning be found?

5. Can you pinpoint anyone around you who seems to manifest this spirit of mockery towards your rebuilding efforts?

6. Outline steps you will take to conquer the onslaught of this spirit in your rebuilding efforts.

Day 44

TACTIC #2: ANGER AND CONSPIRACY

"But it came to pass, that when Sanballat, and Tobiah, and the Arabians, and the Ammonites, and the Ashdodites, heard that the walls of Jerusalem were made up, and that the breaches began to be stopped, then they were very wroth, And conspired all of them together to come and to fight against Jerusalem, and to hinder it." (Nehemiah 4:7-8)

Well, despite all the mockery against the builders of the wall, Nehemiah remained on the wall and refused to meet in the village at the plain of Ono; so the enemy deployed the next line of attack, which was a combination of anger and conspiracy to stop Nehemiah from completing the wall. The enemy is still in the habit of deploying these same tricks. When you refuse to be mocked and remain dedicated to your resolve of building or rebuilding your life, the anger of the adversaries is released towards you.

Take the following exercises as you prepare to overcome this tactic of the enemy:

1. At what point in the battle of destiny do adversaries often resort to anger and conspiracy?

2. Have you ever faced undue antagonism and criticism, even when you were doing the right thing? YES/NO?

3. How do you react when opposed and abandoned by people whom you feel should understand and support you more?

4. Can you mention some people in the Scripture who were criticized and opposed despite being on the right path? One of them is done for you.

a. David.

b.

c.

5. How did the people above react and what can you learn from their various experiences?

Victim of criticism	Reaction	Personal lesson

Day 45

TACTIC #3: TIREDNESS AND LOSS OF VIGOR

"And Judah said, The strength of the bearers of burdens is decayed, and there is much rubbish; so that we are not able to build the wall." (Nehemiah 4:10)

Part of the goals of the enemy is to throw rubble or rubbish along our way, so that we can be discouraged. The enemies did same against Nehemiah and his companions after they had mocked and scorned and unleashed their anger against the builders of the wall. And this time, they succeeded because with these two tactics combined, the willingness and commitment of the builders waned and for a moment the project stopped. The adversaries said to them ten times that they were coming to destroy everything they had done so far and the builders got tired.

Take the following exercises as you receive divine strength in times of discouragement:

1. Point out 5 examples of "rubble" and "rubbish" that the enemy has or can cast in your path as you build or rebuild your life.

a.

b.

c.

d.

e.

2. Cite three passages in the Scripture where God exhorts us that challenges will come but He will help us overcome.

a.

b.

c.

3. Write down examples of 4 individuals in the Scripture on whose destiny path the enemy cast rubble and rubbish but were able to succeed through it all. (Write out the names and the challenges that befell them)

	Name	Challenge
a.		
b.		
c.		
d.		

4. Can you pinpoint the secrets of the success of each of these individuals, despite the enemy's onslaught on them (Write their names and the secrets of their success).

Name	Secret of success
a.	
b.	
c.	
d.	

5. In view of the promises of God and the examples of those who have gone ahead, what should be your attitude when confronted with the rubble and rubbish of life?

Day 46

TACTIC #4: FEAR OF THE ADVERSARY

Being mocked and despised is enough to take a toll on anybody. Especially when combined with anger and conspiracy, it is enough to make anyone consider quitting. The usual response to all of these is fear. Fear is the natural response when we become overwhelmed with our situation. Nehemiah and his men were bullied severely and at one point, they abandoned the work. But Nehemiah encouraged his men to fight; they had their swords, spears, bows in one hand and continued building with the other.

Try these confidence-building exercises as you rebuild:

1. Have you been so discouraged as to quit rebuilding or making efforts to better your life? Now you know you are not alone, nor does it mean you are failure. Make a resolve to resume right away and never to give up anymore.

My Resolve:

2. Fear has been described with a very appropriate acronym. Can you point out what each letter of the word stands for?

F –

E –

A –

R –

3. What is Satan's strategy in making us afraid?

4. What should be your attitude when Satan tries to scare you off your rebuilding effort (See Psalms 23:4 for a clue).

5. Since fear is a spirit and thus transcends what can be physically dealt with, what is the Scripture's prescription for overcoming it (See 2 Timothy 1:7 for a clue).

6. Bible scholars have observed that there are about 365 "fear nots" in the Bible, one for each day of the year. Can you cite 10 of the references containing the "fear not" promise from God?

a.

b.

c.

d.

e.

f.

g.

h.

i.

j.

Day 47

TACTIC #5: PROPAGANDA AS A TOOL OF MANIPULATION

"Then sent Sanballat his servant unto me in like manner the fifth time with an open letter in his hand; Wherein was written, It is reported among the heathen, and Gashmu saith it, that thou and the Jews think to rebel: for which cause thou buildest the wall, that thou mayest be their king, according to these words." (Nehemiah 6:5-6)

The enemy is ever restless but greater is He who is us than the enemy. So, we are guaranteed that we are the ones who will prevail, if we refuse to faint. After several other efforts to frustrate Nehemiah and his helpers had failed, the enemies got increasingly desperate and brutal. Nehemiah was confronted the fifth time with an open letter with surprising accusations. It was written and reported that Nehemiah and his men were about to rebel against the king. It was also said that he was planning to overthrow the king or take over that territory from the king. By any standard, these are serious allegations! But the good news is that Nehemiah was discerning enough to know that it was a strategy of the enemy. I pray that you too will be discerning enough not to give in to the enemy's manipulations.

The following exercises will help you:

1. What do you understand by propaganda?

2. Mention some common forms of propaganda that can be used to discourage someone trying to rebuild their life.

3. Can you recall an instance when the enemies of Jesus used propaganda against Him?

4. Using the examples of Nehemiah and Jesus Christ, how should you react when faced with propaganda?

5. If the enemy had succeeded in weakening you, using the weapon of propaganda, now is the time to resolve to get back on track. Make up your mind to succeed this time!

Day 48

TACTIC #6: FALSE PROPHECY AND DISTRACTION

"And, lo, I perceived that God had not sent him; but that he pronounced this prophecy against me: for Tobiah and Sanballat had hired him." (Nehemiah 6:12)

The enemy, at this stage, seems to have become more creative in his attack against Nehemiah. He delved into an area that requires extraordinary discernment to notice. He got into the garb of a "spirit-filled" person by presenting himself as a messenger of light. Get set for this - when the enemy attempts to distract you and he's not being successful, then he brings forth his last line of attack towards you: False prophecy!

Try these exercises to assess your level of preparation:

1. What does the fact that the enemy tried to use false prophecy to distract Nehemiah teach you about dealing with prophecies generally?

2. What fundamental rule do we have in discerning a true prophecy from a false one?

3. How often do you study God's Word? DAILY/OCCASIONALLY/ONLY IN CHURCH

4. If your answer to the above exercise is not DAILY, resolve, as contained in Joshua 1:8, to make study of God's word a daily activity by preparing a daily Bible reading schedule. For instance, write down a book of the Bible that you will read a chapter from daily, within the next one month.

5. Anything that distracts you from the things of God is dangerous to you. Can you identify certain activities or individuals that distract you from spiritual exercises such as prayer, Bible study or attendance to God's house?

a.

b.

c.

d.

e.

6. Write down steps you will take henceforth to tackle each of these distractions.

Distraction	Steps I will take to tackle it
a.	
b.	
c.	
d.	
e.	

Day 49

UNDER A BETTER COVENANT

"And hath raised us up together, and made us sit together in heavenly places in Christ Jesus:" (Ephesians 2:6)

Our exploration of the life and exploits of Nehemiah has, no doubt, been an enlightening and enriching one. Nehemiah was a strong leader indeed. Yet, his successes were achieved under the Old Testament, which was in many ways limited. Now, we have a new and better covenant, with better promises. Most importantly, we are filled with the Holy Spirit who knows all things, and we have the Lord Jesus Christ who is ever making intercession on our behalves. The implication of all this is that we have a better chance to do even greater exploits and record unprecedented successes in our building and rebuilding efforts.

Try the following exercises as you bask in the blessedness of a better covenant:

1. Christ is the power of the New Covenant and only those who receive Him gain access into its benefits (John 1:12). Have you received Jesus into your life as your Savior and Lord? YES/NO.

2. If your answer to the above is NO, close your eyes now and invite Jesus into your life, surrendering your all to Him.

3. As people under a better covenant, we have more powerful weapons to engage and defeat the enemy. Mention these weapons as listed in Ephesians 6:13-17?

4. Can you explain the significance of each of these weapons to your victory in your building or rebuilding efforts?

5. One powerful distinction in the life of believers under the New Covenant is the availability of gifts from the Holy Spirit, which positions us for greater success in our life's purpose. Have you discovered your gift? YES/NO

6. If your answer to the above is NO, pray for the baptism of the Holy Spirit and ask the Lord to reveal your gift to you.

7. If your answer to exercise 5 is YES, in what ways do you think you can stir up the gift in you for victory in your rebuilding efforts?

a.

b.

c.

Day 50

KINGDOM STEWARDSHIP

"But seek ye first the kingdom of God, and his righteousness; and all these things shall be added unto you." (Matthew 6:33)

Nehemiah was a man with a great heart for God. He did all that he did for the Kingdom's sake; there were no other motives. The condition of the people and the wall drove him to risk even his own life by appearing before the king moody. He did so much for the Kingdom that God promoted him from being a cupbearer to becoming the governor. The challenge for us is: If God could do it in the Old Testament with Nehemiah, how much more will He do it under the better covenant and better promises of this dispensation?

The exercises below will rouse your passion for Kingdom stewardship:

1. What do you understand by "Kingdom stewardship"?

2. Identify 5 ways in which you can contribute to building God's Kingdom.

a.

b.

c.

d.

e

2. How will you personally contribute to God's Kingdom with the above avenues?

a.

b.

c.

d.

e.

3. In what ways can you advance God's Kingdom with the following:

Your talent:

Your spiritual gift:

Your finances:

Your strength:

Your time:

4: List 5 benefits of contributing to God's Kingdom

a.

b.

c.

d.

e.

Day 51

PRAISE AND WORSHIP AS A WEAPON

"Let everything that hath breath praise the Lord. Praise ye the Lord." (Psalms 150:6)

Nehemiah praised God every moment he had the opportunity. He said many times that God should remember him for good (See Nehemiah 5:19, for example). But have you ever wondered—what could make God think about a man? When you praise and worship God, He comes down! The Bible tells us that God inhabits the praises of His people. Every time Nehemiah was delivered from the evil plans of Sanballat and his crew, he offered praise. Many wonders, breakthroughs and victories have been experienced by believers down the ages through the power of praise and worship – and you too can enjoy same today as you build your life.

Take the following exercises on the power of praise and worship:

1. What happens when our praises go up to heaven?

2. Mention three instances in the Scripture where praise and worship brought unprecedented miracles and deliverance to the people of God.

a.

b.

c.

3. Why do you think God is particularly interested in our praise and worship?

4. Think about when last you devoted quality time to praising and worshipping God

5. Determine to devote the entire period of your next prayer time to just praising and worshipping God, without making any personal request.

Day 52

THE MONTH OF ELUL

"So the wall was finished in the twenty and fifth day of the month Elul, in fifty and two days. And it came to pass, that when all our enemies heard thereof, and all the heathen that were about us saw these things, they were much cast down in their own eyes: for they perceived that this work was wrought of our God." (Nehemiah 6:15-16)

Nehemiah was successful in finishing the wall against all odds—in a record time of fifty-two days. He refused to be distracted or bullied off the wall, and it came to pass that his enemies heard that the wall was completed. The Bible records that at the end of the day, his enemies lost their self-confidence. I pray that this will be your testimony as well, as you commit to building or rebuilding your life till it becomes an edifice of immeasurable glory to the name of God and to the shame of Satan.

Take the following exercises to celebrate your triumph!

1. Nehemiah completed the rebuilding of the wall in the month of Elul. What month is the month of Elul in the Jewish tradition and what is the significance?

2. Point out the four ultimate lessons you have derived from the exploit and eventual success of Nehemiah?'

a.

b.

c.

d.

3. Looking at the life of Nehemiah, what do you think will happen if you wholeheartedly commit yourself to rebuilding your life for the glory of God?

4. Make a pledge to God today never to disappoint him in the battle to rebuild your life and fulfill His purpose for you.

5. Write down at least 10 messages that the Holy Spirit has deposited in your heart in the course of attempting these exercises and what you will do about them, beginning from now.

Message	My resolve

a.

b.

c.

e.

f.

g.

h.

i.

6. Set a deadline for yourself within which you must have followed through on all the decisions you have made.

SEE YOU AT THE TOP!

ABOUT THE AUTHOR

Dr. Olalekan Joseph Olowe is a physical therapist by trade and a pastor by calling. Together with his wife, Omolade, they are the Presiding Servants over Kingdom Dominion Ministry International (KDMI) with a ministry base at El Paso, Texas from where they reach out globally.

A graduate of Rocky Mountain University of Health Professionals with a transitional Doctorate in Physical Therapy, Joseph is blessed with a physical therapy practice in El Paso, Texas.

He's a prolific writer and the author of I Am Three Dimensional, Living Free: The Power of Self-Control amongst other books. He's happily married to Omolade and they are blessed with three children.

KINGDOM DOMINION MINISTRY INTERNATIONAL
(KDMI)

To partner with us or to be part of Kingdom Dominion Ministry International (KDMI), please call or write us

1800-561-9170 or +1 915-478-8807

P. O Box 10499
El Paso, TX 79995

info@hisdominion.org | www.hisdominion.org